Beauty For Ashes

By
Arica Clement & Friends Of Faith

Publishing services provided by HelaWrite LLC
& EPIC Books Publishing Indie Division

Cover Design by Oliveri Graphics
Edited and Formatted by Tamar Hela

Summary:

Beauty For Ashes is a compilation of six beautiful, real-life testimonies from women of faith. Arica Clement, the book's creator, was divinely inspired to share her testimony, and encouraged some friends to join her on the journey. These personal stories are heartfelt and display how God revealed Himself in difficult times—how He provided a way out through His Word and healing power. Reading these testimonies will give you hope and a realization that you are not alone in whatever hardship you may be experiencing or have experienced.

Unless otherwise indicated, Scripture quotations in this book are from the New International Version of the Bible

[Non-Fiction-Devotional, Non-Fiction-Christian, Non-Fiction-Inspirational]

ISBN-10: 1941077056
ISBN-13: 978-1-941077-05-4

Dedication

To my father, the late Ronnie R. Jones, who always encouraged me to be myself and to develop a passion for something.

To my grandmother, the late Evelyn J. Jones, who was my first *real* role model.

I love and miss you both dearly—more than words can express.

Acknowledgements

First, I'd like to thank God for giving me the vision of this project, and for providing the provision to complete it. He lined up everything in a way that only He could.

Thanks to Chi, Fernanda, Julie, Lynda, and CeCe for accepting the call and having the courage to share their stories to encourage others.

Special thanks to my editor and publisher, Tamar, who worked her editing talents on each of these testimonies. I thank you for your honesty and encouragement during every step of this project.

To my husband, Anthony: Thank you for standing with me, and always supporting my dreams and aspirations.

To my children: Amaya, AJ, and Austin. I can't imagine being without you three. Thank you for keeping my life exciting and action-filled.

Thanks to Mr. Odis for lighting a fire underneath me and encouraging me to do my best at all costs.

And lastly, to my sister, Paula: Thanks for all your love and support. We are more alike than not. I thank God for restoring all that was lost in our childhood.

Table of Contents

Sunshine After The Rain

Chi Abraham-Igwe

"Rejoice in the Lord always. I will say it again:
Rejoice!" Philippians 4:4

Introduction

It is a very painful experience to lose a family member, a friend, or anyone, for that matter. Even when we think we are prepared, we end up feeling torn apart because death comes with such finality.

Ever sat down, wishing the day never existed? That yesterday would remain and continue to exist? Just one more day, we say… We are never prepared, especially when we feel that a loved one has been taken so young, or in their prime.

I had a dear friend in her 90's, who was in great pain, and had asked me to pray for her so that she could go home to be with the Lord. Now *that* was someone who was ready. She had done her work here on Earth, but even then, how does one pray such a prayer? I simply prayed, "Let your will be done Lord…" She went home to be with the Lord about a month later.

It's been a few years now, but we still miss her. If you've experienced losing a loved one, then you know that the reality that we will never talk to that person again, nor feel the warmth of their embrace, suddenly hits so hard.

In 1997, I lost my mom—a very dear and precious Christian woman. I had spent Easter weekend with her before leaving for the city where I worked. Two days later, I received a call that she was sick. She had actually passed on early that morning, but they didn't want to tell me the news over the phone. So, I was instead told that she was very sick and that I needed to be home.

The news of her passing was so painful; it felt like my heart was being ripped away from me. During our very last weekend together, I had introduced my (now) husband to her, not knowing that she would never live to see me get married. That she would never hold any of my children, nor be by my side during labor.

Seeing my dad then, who now has also passed away, as he wept, tore me apart. I had never before seen him cry. As I wailed, I wanted to go to the morgue and pray, laying hands on her so that she would come back to life. I was still in my 20's; it was a very dark time for me.

Words That Comfort

The one thing that kept me going was my mom's last words. She had told my younger sister, who was with her as she took her last breath, "Tell them I am going home." Mom knew she was going to be with the Lord! God used those last words to bring comfort to my aching heart. As I put these words into writing, I still become teary-eyed because she is no longer here to give me a hug, which she loved to give, or to fast and pray with me. She was my very first prayer partner, and I miss her so much.

In the face of grief, we mourn and weep, and do not want to wake up to the next day. Food becomes tasteless and we wonder: *How can I make it through the day?* I pondered these things as we planned her funeral. God saw me through that time of darkness. He lifted me and took the weight off me. He wiped my tears away and turned my sorrow to joy.

"...weeping may remain for a night, but rejoicing comes in the morning." Psalm 30:5

"Brothers, we do not want you to be ignorant about those who fall asleep, or to grieve like the rest of men, who have no hope. We believe that Jesus died and rose again and so we believe that God will bring with Jesus those who have fallen asleep in him."
1 Thessalonians 4:13-14

The above are some of the verses that kept me going, as well as the knowledge that Mom was home with the Lord.

And It Strikes Again!

About a year after my husband and I were married, we found out that we were going to have a baby. We were so thrilled, and I quickly spread the good news. 10 weeks into that pregnancy, I started bleeding and it wouldn't stop. This ended up in a very painful miscarriage, as we both watched the life that was growing inside me become nonexistent.

When we find ourselves in a difficult situation, we should always remember that God has not left us. He is our Shepherd, walking with us, and His banner over us is love. God alone has the answers to our questions. We may never find the "why," nor the answers we want, but we must remember that His plans for us are of good, and not of evil—just like the Word tells us in Jeremiah 29:11.

God saw us through that time as we encouraged ourselves with His words. Are *you* hurting from the loss of your unborn child? Remember: He gave breath to that life in the first place, and He is more than able to do it again.

It was the end of summer in 2000, when we discovered we were expecting again, and I had just moved to Europe. My husband was in the U.S., and I could not join him, as my visa was not yet ready. We were both so thrilled at the news of the baby, but I still had some mixed feelings; first, because I was thousands of miles away from my husband, and second, because of my experience with the previous pregnancy, which had ended after 10 weeks. I was filled with fear of the unknown. The Enemy tries to plant seeds of fear in our hearts, using past events. We just have to reach for that Word, get a hold of it, and let *it* get a hold of us.

"Every good and perfect gift is from above, coming down from the Father of the heavenly lights, who does not change like shifting shadows." James 1:17 This Scripture got a hold of me, and I started rejoicing in what the Lord had done in my life.

I also encouraged myself with the words of **Matthew 6:25-34, "Therefore I tell you, do not worry about your life, what you will eat or drink; or about your body, what you will wear. Is not life more important than** food, and the body more important than clothes? Look at the birds of the air; they do not sow or reap or store away in barns, and yet your heavenly Father feeds them. Are you not much more valuable than they? Who of you by worrying can add a single hour to his life?

And why do you worry about clothes? See how the lilies of the field grow. They do not labor or spin. Yet I tell you that not even Solomon in all his splendor was dressed like one of these. If that is how God clothes the grass of the field, which is here today and tomorrow is thrown into the fire, will he not much more clothe you, O you of little faith? So do not worry, saying, 'What shall we eat?' or 'What shall we drink?' or 'What shall we wear?' For the pagans run after all these things, and your heavenly Father knows that you need them. But seek first his kingdom and his righteousness, and all these things will be given to you as well. Therefore do not worry about tomorrow, for tomorrow will worry about itself. Each day has enough trouble of its own."

As the due date neared, my husband flew in from California, where he was then living and working, to be with me. The date came and passed, with no signs of labor. A week after, still no sign. I was becoming very impatient and just wanted the pregnancy to be over with. We both watched as our friend, who was also pregnant at the same time, have her baby; we just couldn't wait to hold our baby in our arms.

Beauty For Ashes

The Nightmare

Then came the morning of May fifteenth, about two days shy of forty-two weeks, I woke up and noticed some bleeding. We went to the emergency room to check this out. We met with the doctor, and she said the bleeding was just a heavy show. I had read about the "show" in my pregnancy book, but not a heavy show. In my ignorance, I thought: *Well, she is the one who went to medical school and knows her stuff, so who am I to question?* I was then admitted into the hospital.

Eight hours later, I had barely dilated three centimeters. By that time however, my water had broken, but no one seemed to have known when that had happened. I was so tired from the pain and contractions that I barely noticed I was laying in a pool of my own blood. My husband quickly alerted the nurses because we didn't think things were progressing, as they should have been.

They quickly rushed me into the operating room for an emergency C-section. I was so overwhelmed with fear and was praying it would all end well. My husband was not allowed in the operating room with me. I had never felt so alone.

Lying there on the table, I had no idea when the baby came, because I did not hear a sound, and no one said a word to me. As I weakly turned my head around, I saw them trying to resuscitate a baby, and I weakly mumbled, "Is that my baby?" and was told yes.

15

The baby eventually gave a very weak cry. We were told that she had to be in the ICU, and not with me. I was then put in a ward with other new moms. It was so painful to watch as these moms had their little cots with their babies by their bedside. It was a difficult time hearing those babies cry, and watching them being nursed, while I suffered from the pain of the surgery and no joy of holding a baby.

Finally, we were able to go see our daughter in the intensive care unit. She had all sorts of tubes attached to her little body, and looked so helpless as she tugged at her dad's finger. We wished we could turn things around; we could only touch her and not hold her. She was on antibiotics, and we were told she had swallowed a lot of meconium in utero, and that because the placenta separated, she had also suffered some oxygen loss. The doctor told us that even if she survived, she would be a vegetable.

Almost three days after she was born, she was gone. We never got to hold her, nurse her, change her, or cuddle her. I remember holding her lifeless body in my arms, and crying out to God to restore life to her. It was the first time I had held her, and it was her lifeless body. I didn't know what to do.

We both held her as we cried out to God—so many questions unanswered, the feeling of helplessness. We were in a country where we barely knew anyone. It was like a bad dream as the nurse said to bring what we would like to bury her in, while we started making funeral arrangements.

"Even though I walk through the valley of the shadow of death, I will fear no evil for you are with me..." Psalm 23:4

Although we were hurting very much, we knew that God was with us. He had gone ahead of us, because He is such an amazing God. In this land where we knew no one, God had actually gone ahead of us. A very close family friend had introduced us to a young couple who was pastoring a church in the city we happened to be in. We had gone and worshipped with them before that time, and the sweet lady had given us gifts for the baby.

When they heard what had happened, they quickly came and took us both from the hospital and put us in a very nice hotel. They became our family, and helped us organize the funeral. God also made a way for our close friends in London to come and be with us. We were hurting so much, and having these lovely people around us was such a blessing.

This made **Romans 8:38-39** so real to me: **"For I am convinced that neither death nor life, neither angels nor demons, neither the present nor the future, nor any powers, neither height nor depth, nor anything else in all creation, will be able to separate us from the love of God that is in Christ Jesus our Lord."** God used those people to surround us with love.

On the day of the funeral, my husband and I went to

see our little girl one more time before the casket was closed. I can still see her sweet little face; she was in the dress I had bought for her to wear when we left the hospital. As the tiny white casket was being lowered into the ground; we wept. Words cannot describe the pain in my heart that day. I felt so empty, so robbed. I had gone through those nine months and came out empty-handed.

Facing the reality of it all was devastating. Being that I was still waiting for my visa to join my husband in the States, I could not be with him—like we hadn't suffered enough! Now, we had to bear the pain thousands of miles apart. If there was one thing that kept me going, it was hearing my husband tell me that it was a miracle I hadn't died in that hospital bed.

Many times, it's hard to see ahead. It's difficult to look beyond the immediate problem, circumstance, or situation we find ourselves in. I could not see *tomorrow* in the midst of my pain. But God was able and gave me a reason to start being thankful. I locked in on what my husband had said to me: "It's a miracle you didn't die in that bed." I became thankful that I had not died, and thankful that I had survived the ordeal. After all, only a living person could have another child. I stopped asking questions and began to see ahead—that some day, I would be a mom and needed to stand strong and get past this to be one. God is the One who makes a way when there seems to be no way.

It is very important that, as we go through trials, or whatever comes our way, we understand that things, which do not go the way we anticipated, do not make God a liar or a failure. So many situations that come our way in life cannot be explained or be understood, but like the apostle Paul says, "We will understand it better by and by." So we move on, trusting, and knowing that He who has made promises is faithful.

Moving On

I had my good and bad days as I tried to move on. I knew God had not given up on me, so I couldn't give up on myself. I gathered all the baby stuff we had bought for our little girl and boxed it up, believing that someday, my future daughter would use them!

The waiting period for my visa continued. God, who sees ahead, had used the president at that time to pass a law, allowing spouses who had waited for a particular length of time to join their significant others, using a new class of visa. In July of the same year, I was able to join my husband. This miracle of reuniting with him made my healing process go faster. It brought new joy. The following year, we were blessed with a beautiful baby girl, and then later, with two handsome boys. God wiped away all our tears.

My dear friend, I don't know what blows life has dealt you. Perhaps you are facing the loss of a child, a spouse, parent, relative, a dear friend. I can't tell you that I know how you feel, because I really do not know. I can only share how I felt, and how God saw me through. I can confidently say that if He did it for me—who is so unworthy—then He can do it for you.

Remember, the Holy Spirit is the Comforter. Invite Him to invade your space. Open up your heart to Him and feel the warmth of His embrace. Find the verse that speaks to your heart, and hold on to it. Post it on your refrigerator, doors, and cars. **"Give thanks to the Lord, for he is good. His love endures forever." Psalm 136:1** No matter what you are going through, His love never fails! When I feel alone, I always pray: Lord Jesus, let me feel the warmth of your embrace; wrap your arms around me, sweet Holy Spirit.

Friend, you can take that step through your hurt and pain. He does not want us to do this journey alone. That is why He sent His son, Jesus Christ. Do I still have worries and worry every now and again? The answer is: yes! In times like this, I go to the Word. Therein, I find comfort and guidance. I find hope for tomorrow through it. Don't give up on yourself. Rise up! God is on your side. He can turn things around for you. Just believe.

Restoration

Arica Clement

"...to comfort all who mourn,
and provide for those who grieve in Zion—to
bestow on them a crown of beauty
instead of ashes,
the oil of gladness
instead of mourning,
and a garment of praise
instead of a spirit of despair.
They will be called oaks of righteousness,
a planting of the LORD
for the display of his splendor."
Isaiah 61:2-3

Beauty For Ashes

Introduction

When I thought about writing my testimony, I was excited because God was telling me—*calling* me—to share my story. It may not be an intense drama that someone might be expecting, but it's real, true, and heartfelt. And it's long overdue. *What if it's never published* was one of the questions that came up. Well, it doesn't matter. It is written. God has given me the courage, the words, and the strength to put my story, my truth, on paper.

A box full of painful memories will have to be opened. The hearts of others will have to be prepared to receive these truths that have been painstakingly written down through tears. Those are a couple of facts that came before me as I was contemplating what parts of my life's testimony could be shared. God will give me strength through it all. I know that I am His and He is mine.

He said to me, **"...I have chosen you and have not rejected you." Isaiah 41:9** And this is what gives me the courage, strength, and faith to forge ahead. He allows me to be transparent, so that others will be encouraged and reminded that they are not alone in whatever trial they're experiencing. That they will know that God is with them, loves them, and wants to save them.

"Trust in the Lord with all your heart and lean not on your own understanding; in all your ways acknowledge him, and he will make your paths straight." Proverbs 3:5-6

Beauty For Ashes

A Lost Relationship

My first memories are from the age of three. My maternal grandmother resided in Ocean Springs, Mississippi, which is a coastal town with an Air Force base stationed there. With a coin in my hand, I proceeded to walk across a railroad track to the local grocery store to buy a lollipop.

When I returned to my grandmother's house, nothing had changed. It was a regular day. Her house was a temporary place for me to stay until my paternal grandmother—Ma—could pick me up. She lived in East Palo Alto, California, along with her son—my father— who was in the military.

When Ma arrived to get me, we went shopping. She purchased a new blue dress and white walking shoes for me to wear on the airplane ride back to California. It was my first time flying in an airplane, but not my last. There would be one other round-trip flight, made from California to Mississippi, before the trips stopped. There are few people outside of my family who know this story, until now.

When I was conceived, my father was in the Air Force, stationed in Ocean Springs, Mississippi. My mother lived in the same town. They were never married. Not knowing that my father was expecting a child, Ma received a letter in the mail from him. The letter said he was now a father, and he gave her my name and birth weight. He was very excited. (Many years later, Ma gave me the letter, and it's still in my possession today.)

And so the story goes. I lived with my mother until my grandmother intervened and contacted Ma to say that I was not being properly cared for. My father and Ma made a decision that she would travel to Ocean Springs to get me.

A couple of days after her arrival, we traveled by airplane to California. Ma's house was my home during the week, and my father's house was home on the weekends. I stayed in California for about a year. And then my mother wanted me back.

My stay with my mother was short. Not long after being reunited with her, Ma was contacted again by my other grandmother. So, it was back to California. Once again, my time in California with my dad and Ma was threatened when my mother contacted them, wanting me to be returned to Ocean Springs.

My dad and Ma were both very upset. My father had become attached to me and could not bear to lose me again. Ma had also become attached to me, but was tired of flying back and forth on a moment's notice.

During that time, Ma was working at the VA hospital. One of her patients had a son who was an attorney. Papers were drawn up to keep me in California and were sent to my mother. We didn't hear from her again for 10 years. Meanwhile, my father got married and I lived with him and my stepmother. Ma relocated to the

Beauty For Ashes

Sacramento area.

One year, while I was away at summer camp, my mother called. Upon my return home, my father said that my mother had called and that I needed to call her back. So, I sat down to call her. We had a short conversation, which ended with her asking if I wanted to come and live with her. Of course, I said yes. I had always wondered what it would be like to experience a mother-daughter relationship that I'd only witnessed through other people.

After our conversation ended, my father asked me what we talked about. I told him the part about going to live with my mother. He was not happy about the idea of me wanting to go live with my mother. Surprisingly, he called her right back to say that me living with her was not an option, and would not be considered until my 18th birthday—when I would be able to decide for myself whether or not to live with her.

The devastation of not having a relationship with my mother was very painful. My dad and Ma loved me dearly, and my feelings for them were mutual, but it didn't matter. There was still a void that I felt was not filled. I wanted to know my mother and have a relationship with her. Feelings of emptiness surrounded me because there was a longing for my mother that would never be fulfilled.

Looking back now, there was a deep sadness in my heart that led me to experiencing depression. No one could fill that empty space. As a child, I didn't understand why my mother didn't love me, or want me to be with her.

There wasn't a rebuttal against what my heart believed to be true. When people would say that my mother didn't want me, I believed them. There wasn't any evidence to prove otherwise. I was a victim of circumstance—an innocent child who had become an inconvenience. Because I was so young when this happened, the hurt I felt didn't surface until I was much older.

The anger and pain I experienced because of my mother was emptied into a little hypothetical box and stored into the back of my thoughts. That was my way of managing the emotions I felt but could not express. Every now and then, I would think of her, but for the most part, my heart had resolved to be content with the love given to me by my dad and Ma. And it was good.

I was 15 when I accepted Christ into my heart. It happened one summer when I was away at summer camp. I'd gone to this particular camp several times over the years. I found out about the camp through a Bible study I attended. The couple who facilitated the Bible study also worked for the Christian organization that ran the camp. The Bible study was where I first began to learn about God and His gift of salvation. I learned a lot, but always left the Bible study with questions. Too embarrassed to ask, my questions remained unanswered.

Throughout the years, I accepted Jesus into my heart many times, but I never felt *transformed*. This may sound silly, but I thought something magical would happen when I accepted Christ into my heart. However, nothing did. The words I had spoken to become "Saved" and "Born

Again" were real. I believed every one of them, yet my heart wasn't changed. I left the Bible study feeling the same way I did when I had walked in.

That summer was different, though. God revealed to me that accepting Him was more than just speaking words. He began to show me how He saw me. He began to bring people into my life who could answer my questions. I felt encouraged. That was my first time experiencing God.

Tragedy Strikes

It was the end of June when my dad came to visit. The summer of the previous year, I had moved to Sacramento with Ma. My dad rode the Greyhound bus from East Palo Alto to Sacramento, and called me to pick him up once he arrived. It was a surprise. We weren't expecting him, but were both very happy that he'd come. The last time I'd seen him had been in May, shortly after my twentieth birthday. Although we all had a good time visiting with each other and catching up, he seemed to be melancholy.

We talked the way we always had. He was telling stories and making me laugh. My dad had always been laid back and easy going—not the typical father some might expect. He would dance in front of me and my friends, tell jokes, dress up for Halloween, and even talk to me about boys. He was fun. But something was different. There was a seriousness about him that I'd never before seen. Something in his eyes had changed.

Beauty For Ashes

A few days later, Ma had to work, so I took my dad to the Greyhound station so that he could return home. Taken over by emotions, my tears started to flow while saying goodbye. My heart was sad to see him go. It was as if I knew it would be the last time we would see each other.

A few weeks after my dad had come to visit, Ma and I received life-changing news that would forever alter our lives. I remember the moment like it was yesterday.

It was July 1990. I was getting ready to go to a funeral service for a friend of mine. We had become friends while attending the same local junior college. My cousin called to say that his mother, my aunt, was on her way over. This was strange because my aunt lived in San Jose, and I lived in Sacramento with Ma. (It's also about a two-hour drive from one place to the other.) She did not give any notice or call; she was just on her way. But my mind was on other things.

Knowing that my day was already planned, and Ma was off work that day, someone would be home to meet her when she arrived. My cousin asked me to wait for her to get there, and his voice was very solemn. Time didn't permit me to stop long enough to question what was happening. Soon, everything became clear.

While I was taking a shower, I heard a scream. Not the scream of someone being physically hurt, but the scream of heartache and anguish and of a heart breaking. There was some commotion and then movement towards the bathroom. They were right outside the bathroom door calling my name. The voices belonged to Ma and my aunt.

My aunt's voice was very clear, and Ma's voice silenced as my aunt began to speak. She said, "Arica, he's gone, he's gone."

And I asked, "What? Who's gone?"

She replied back, "Your father's gone. He's been killed."

At that very moment, everything went dark. It was as if time stood still. Every part of me went numb. All the feeling in my body was gone, and it seemed as though it was all happening in slow motion. But in reality, it was just seconds. And that's when the pain came. It felt like my heart was penetrated by blunt force. The pain was so great, it brought me down to my knees and I began to cry. "They killed him, they killed him, they killed him." Those were the only words coming out of my mouth.

Sorrow had overtaken me. No one had ever prepared me for the death of my dad. I felt heartbroken beyond belief. *This is what it feels like to lose someone you love?* Not just anybody, but *my dad.* We shared a bond—a special connection between father and daughter. And now, that connection had been severed, and there was nothing I could do to repair it. Then, fear set in. *What would happen to me? How would I get through this?*

There I was, 20 years old, and my father hadn't been

killed by cancer or a car accident, but was murdered by street violence—taken by the hands of someone young enough to be his son. Devastation was an understatement. The only person who had loved me more than anybody was gone. Initially, I was angry and could not understand why God had allowed this to happen. During that time, He didn't give me any answers, but He did give me comfort and hope that I would be all right. Although he was no longer with me, I knew that my memories of my dad would last my entire lifetime, and be shared with my children, and their children, through stories and pictures.

"The Lord himself goes before you and will be with you; he will never leave you nor forsake you. Do not be afraid; do not be discouraged." Deuteronomy 31:8

Now, as time has passed, the pain in my heart has lessened. The hollow part inside of me has been slowly filled. It didn't all happen at once, but was a work in progress. My spirit was broken, yet God repaired my brokenness, and restored my joy.

With nowhere else to turn, I sought God. He was my safe haven when there was no escape from the pain and the hurt that came along with losing my dad. He gave me peace in the midst of everything going on around me, and gave me hope. God wrapped His arms around me and comforted me when no one else could.

"The Lord is close to the brokenhearted and saves those who are crushed in spirit." Psalm 34:18

Beauty For Ashes

A New Start

A few years after my dad died, Ma retired from nursing and moved back to her hometown in Arkansas, and I transferred to San Jose State University to continue my education. My college roommate was one of my best friends from high school. We both attended San Jose State. Three times a week, I attended classes, and on the other two days, I worked as teller for a bank's cash vault. It was then that I began to seek God.

My cousin was a member of a church in Fremont and invited me to attend their Sunday service. This church had a lot of young people, and a pastor who was energetic and charismatic. The environment was warm and welcoming. It felt like home. As a child and young person, I had had feelings of being disconnected—like I wasn't a part of anything. I had always felt like there was no place for me. But being in this new community was the first time that God had given me confirmation that my place was with His family.

God began to slowly reveal Himself through His Word because of my obedience through prayer. I would always begin my prayers by thanking God for Jesus Christ, who died on the cross for me. What a gift! *Am I worthy of it?* No, but God believes that I am. So, my wanting to please Him originated from the sacrifice. The desire of my heart, at the time, was to be humble, selfless, and have a love for people. He changed me. These prayers were life-altering because they allowed me to let down my guard and begin to trust people again.

Although my personality was very outgoing and I was known to be talkative, the circumstances of my childhood had left me guarded and distrusting. But God turned it all around. One of the scriptures I memorized and meditated on during that time was in the book of Psalm.

"Create in me a pure heart, O God, and renew a steadfast spirit within me. Do not cast me from your presence or take your Holy Spirit from me. Restore to me the joy of your salvation and grant me a willing spirit, to sustain me." Psalm 51:10-12

As time went on, my relationship with the Lord grew. A new confidence had replaced the old feelings of detachment and doubt. And I didn't forget where He'd brought me from, either. Life was going well. I was the first in my immediate family to graduate from college. The dedication and hard work had paid off. My boyfriend and I had become engaged and purchased a home to live in after we were married. We were preparing ourselves to have children also. Wow! God had restored the joy that was once lost and had transformed my whole life, mind, body, and soul. But our minds are full of old memories that have a way of reminding us of past matters we'd rather forget.

When I was preparing to have children, feelings of abandonment resurfaced, and that little box I'd put all my pain and hurt into so many years ago was reopened. It was similar to a floodgate being opened. Panic set in. *How could this be happening?* I thought to myself. I realized that I had never allowed God to heal the one area of my life that was still broken and causing pain: the broken relationship with my mother.

In my own strength, there wasn't a resolution or a way to fix what was broken. God revealed Himself in a mighty way when the burden was given to Him. Prayer works, and God provided a way out. Through prayer and fasting, He revealed that I needed to forgive my mother for not being a part of my life. Forgiveness would be the only way God would allow me to be a good mother to my own children. It was the only way to have freedom from the hurt and pain.

With God's prompting, I sat down to write my mother a letter. The choice had been made to forgive her without an explanation. Knowing why she made the decision not to keep me was not a prerequisite to my being able to forgive her. If an explanation were needed, then my heart wouldn't have been sincere. Instead, I chose to honor my mother, regardless of the nature of our relationship.

God gave me peace and freedom from the hurt my heart carried. It was truly a burden lifted. There was a release from the bondage that had held me. I was free to be a good mother to my children. The reality of it all is that my mother was the best mother I could have ever had. If things had been different, God would not have allowed me to be the person I am today. I thank Him for His timing because, as a young person, my heart and mind were not spiritually prepared to forgive. He had to chisel away the stuff surrounding my heart to get the darkness out and allow the light to come in.

"Honor your father and mother—which is the first commandment with a promise—that it may go well with you and that you may enjoy long life on the earth." Ephesians 6:2-3

Losing Ma

Ma passed away in January of 2010. She battled a rare form of stomach cancer for the last five years of her life. When she had told me that she was diagnosed with cancer, I had hope. Hope that she would be healed and restored, because a cancer diagnosis today isn't what it was twenty years ago.

While pregnant with my third child, I traveled to Chicago to visit Ma while she underwent chemotherapy. After going through a series of chemotherapy treatments, the cancer did not go into remission. That was when the worry set in. Even though Ma was my grandmother, she was like a mother—*my* mother. The only mother I'd ever known. My heart could not take losing another person who was such a huge part of my life.

We were very close. We talked on the phone with one another at least once a week. She was strong, giving, and independent. And she had stood up for me many times in my life. She was wise in all the ways grandmothers are, with comforting and encouraging words that always lifted me up when I was feeling discouraged.

Beauty For Ashes

Ma's passing was expected, but still hard on my family. Being able to see her to say goodbye and spend some quiet time alone with her provided closure for me. She was receiving hospice care in Chicago where she lived with my aunt. My husband and I made the decision that it was time for me to fly out to see her and say my goodbyes. That time was much different than the last. She was not the same person who welcomed me with a big smile and hug. And her boisterous laugh was silent.

When I arrived to my aunt's house, she led me upstairs to Ma's room, which was filled with loved ones. She was asleep and my aunt woke her up to tell her I was there. When she opened her eyes, she looked over at me and we just stared at each other. I held on to her hand, and she blinked her eyes. My aunt asked her if she knew who I was. She said, "Yeah, I know Arica." I just smiled and leaned down to hug her.

That was the last time I heard her speak. It was on a Friday. Over the next few days, other family members came into town to also say their goodbyes. We all spent some private time alone with her. She was truly loved— and the matriarch of my family. I returned home the following Tuesday, and Ma passed away on Wednesday. The peace of the Lord came over me, because she was home.

Words cannot begin to express how God carried me through this. The peace He gave me outweighed everything that comes with losing a loved one. Until it happened, there was disbelief that I could even handle a life-altering loss again. Now I'd lost two people who loved me the most. But God's love and never-changing hand are amazing. He gave me comfort through it all.

There was a peace in my heart that was different in me than when my dad had died. My grandmother would appear to me in dreams, and they were always happy ones. Most of the dreams left me remembering only segments, but that was okay. Joy overcame me because I realized that she was all right. She was free. All the pain and suffering were gone, and the spiritual transformation had occurred. This was the beginning of me experiencing a higher level of who God was and is, and I had a better understanding of His Word. There was also the realization that His plans for our lives are perfect, whether we believe it or not. He knew us before we even came to be.

"My frame was not hidden from you when I was made in the secret place. When I was woven together in the depths of the earth, your eyes saw my unformed body. All the days ordained for me were written in your book before one of them came to be." Psalm 139:15-16

Going Forward

Currently, my husband and I have been married for 16 years. We have one daughter and two sons. Although my relationship with all three of my children is valued and healthy, the bond my daughter and I share is a godsend. All the heartache and hurt endured by not having a relationship with my own mother has solidified the connection between my daughter and myself. In other words, God has allowed me to be a good mother despite the brokenness that existed between my mother and me.

God is the center of my life. I seek Him in all things, and I praise Him for everything—in the big things and small things. And even in the trials, because without them, we don't grow. He wants to grow us. We have to search and seek Him out through His Word. When we think no one is there, He is right there with us. I've learned to trust Him especially when I don't understand, because I have faith and know that His plans for my life are perfect.

Please don't misunderstand; I struggle and experience obstacles and deal with life's challenges, just like everyone else. But I ask God for help. I lean on Him. I stay spiritually connected to the Father, so I can grow. It's like lifting weights: the more you do it, the stronger you become. The stronger you become, the heavier the weights get. I can do nothing in my own strength, but can do anything through Christ Jesus. The Holy Spirit is amazing.

God wants us to have an intimate relationship with Him. He will come in and transform your heart, mind, body, and soul. There's just one catch: You have to invite Him in to your life. God wants you to invite Him in, so that you can experience all that He has for you and more. He's a gentleman, and will not force his way in. Instead, He gives you a choice.

"Now faith is being sure of what we hope for and certain of what we do not see." Hebrews 11:1

"I can do everything through him who gives me strength." Philippians 4:13

Overcoming Is A Journey To Victory

Kathlene Delgado

"...God has made me fruitful in the land of my suffering." Genesis 41:52

Beauty For Ashes

A Chapter of My Life's Journey

June 26, 2002 As I lay strapped to the spinal board, numb from my neck all the way to my feet, I could hear the sirens screaming through intersections, the ambulance rushing me to the hospital. Friends and family only knew that I was in Nashville, Tennessee, nearly 3,000 miles away from my home in San Jose, California. They had no idea where I was in that very moment.

As the ambulance sped through intersections, I had a flashback as clear as the moment I was in: I was sitting in the sanctuary of Celebration Community Church where I was a very involved member. It was located on a busy street in San Jose. Fire trucks and ambulances would frequently speed by with their sirens blaring. Our Pastor, Dr. Gregory Babish, had taught us to simply raise our hands toward the passing ambulance or fire truck and silently bless them.

Many times, Pastor would also raise his hand toward the emergency vehicles and pray from the pulpit, "Lord, protect them and give them wisdom in the emergency situation they are in…" never skipping a beat from his message! It was never a big deal or an interruption to our services. It was a simple prayer and gesture for the situation, which was totally known to God, but unknown to any of us.

Back in my "moment," I was in an ambulance with loud sirens, speeding to a hospital in a city that I had never been in. I knew there had to be someone out there, raising their hand toward that ambulance and praying for me, for the drivers, and for the wisdom of my caretakers to handle emergency decisions that were being made on my behalf.

My thoughts were interrupted by the radio transmission as the EMT gave my vitals to the ER dispatcher. They had already started an IV, and applied an oxygen mask to my face; my blood pressure was dropping, and I was going into shock. The dispatcher rerouted us from the nearest hospital to Nashville Baptist Hospital, which was further away but had immediate space available. The closest ER had been filled with car accident victims.

Fifteen minutes later, we arrived at Nashville Baptist Hospital, and I was rushed into the ER. Although in shock, I never lost consciousness. Without trying to sound super spiritual, I withdrew into myself, away from the unknown, away from the chaos and drama, away from fear and a lot of questions for which I had absolutely no answers.

I began singing children's church praise songs in my head, and amazingly stayed focused on the Lord. He was with me, and Proverbs 18:24 truly became a living experience: **"One who has unreliable friends soon comes to ruin, but there is a friend who sticks closer than a brother."** And that Friend is Jesus Christ, the Son of the living God, Who was sticking to me that very hour and in all seasons of my life!

This particular season appeared to be a tragic accident, but would soon show that it was God's divine intervention for a new beginning of His purpose for my life. I would once again become fruitful for Him.

Speaking of the "beginning," let me start at the beginning! That's always a good place to start!

In January of the same year—2002—I knew it was going to be the beginning of a brand new year, new season, and new chapter in my life's journey. I had been through two horrific seasons of personal betrayal, from 1991 through 2001, which not only shook my world but also took my breath away—each individual nearly broke my heart, my soul, and my spirit.

I felt like Joseph, son of Jacob, when his brothers had sold him into slavery. 2002 was the year and time that I called out: "It is finished; rise up and move on!" God promised it to me and I was ready...or so, I thought.

This part of my life's journey and testimony that I share here has to do with what happens when we receive a promise from God and think we are waiting upon the Lord, but we step out or jump too soon and realize it was "our will in God's name" not "His will in His name." How can one know this? Because of the fruit that is produced from poor choices! Don't you hate it when that happens? But, praise God; His promises are true and I still cling to **Isaiah 61:3, "...and provide for those who grieve in Zion—to bestow on them a crown of beauty instead of ashes, the oil of gladness instead of mourning, and a garment of praise instead of a spirit of despair. They will be called oaks of righteousness, a planting of the**

LORD for the display of his splendor."

Pastor Babish calls those times the "in between times." The time between a promise or prophecy is given to the time that it is realized in its "fullness of time." Woe to us when we jump too quickly, and don't wait on the Lord. I was in one of those "in between times," and jumped too quickly, because I wanted to be out of the sorrow and pain I was in at the time. Everything seemed to be lining up perfectly (or I wanted to believe so), but I could not have been more wrong. My loving Heavenly Father, however, took me through the valley of the shadow of death so that I could learn the lessons He had for me.

I received a long distance phone call from friends who were Fine Arts pastors. I had done many large productions with them in San Jose. They had relocated to a mega-church in a suburb of Nashville, Tennessee. I had just finished my certification and internship at San Jose State University, and was ready for the "new" in my life, with production work through "Events." I had been a licensed Children's Pastor since 1985 and loved every moment, but I wanted to move on to something different, something fresh, and something new. After all, God wouldn't want me to waste all my creative talents, would He?

My friends asked if I would fly to Tennessee around the 4th of July and help create a 4th of July production at their church. I said I would pray about it, and I did. My friend and mentor in San Jose, Pat Babish, prayed with me through all the decisions that were coming up. The trip was being planned for late June to do the production, and then I would go on to Asheville, North Carolina, to visit my mother for 10 days.

As time went on, plans for flights were made and confirmed. In mid-May, the Fine Arts pastor called to ask if I would be interested in relocating to Tennessee, and to apply for the position of his Administrator/Assistant in the Fine Arts Department at their church! I thought: *WOW...this is it...my ticket out of California, to start fresh, somewhere new!* I quickly agreed, and said I would send my résumé for him to set up an interview at the end of June when I arrived in Nashville to do the production.

At that moment, I stepped out of the will of God. Although I called it "His Will," hindsight tells me clearly that it was: "My will; not His." The first red flag was when I was asked: "How would you like to apply for the Fine Arts Administrator position?" I immediately blurted a resounding, "YES!" I never prayed about it, but instead ran to my friend and mentor, Pat, and told her about the amazing doors God was opening for me! As always, she prayed with me for God's doors to be clearly opened, and for doors to be clearly shut tight if they were not truly opportunities for me in "His will." She encouraged me to remember to: "...be still, and know He is God."

The months passed quickly, and I was excited for the imagined new start, finally being able to put all the pain of the past behind me. Hallelujah! I packed, and all appeared ready and organized to leave. On Saturday, June 22nd, I boarded the plane from San Jose International Airport for Nashville, Tennessee. I was full of excitement and anticipation of "The Promised Land!"

All too soon, I would find out that running away from pain is actually called "denial." The only escape from that is to face the pain and problems as Jesus did in facing His Cross. It was the way of the Cross that would become the actual, genuine redemption of self-centered destruction from the past, a.k.a. *sin*. The way of the Cross is **Mark 8:34**, when Jesus said: **"If anyone would come after me, he must deny himself and take up his cross and follow me."**

I arrived in Nashville, and connected with my friends. We discussed the week's plan for the production, and then began the actual work. My interviews were to begin Tuesday, and I was ready for them. However, as I worked diligently on the production Sunday and Monday, I began to sense that I would not be a good fit there. I was born and raised in Santa Cruz, California, and being in Tennessee was a whole different world! The culture was (for lack of a better phrase) a "Good Ol' Boys Environment." It was a literal culture shock for this California Girl!

I chose to cancel the employment interviews, not without disappointment from my Fine Arts pastor friends. Nevertheless, I knew in my heart of hearts that I did not belong in Tennessee long-term, or that I should have made it my new home. Free from that burden, I continued on the production, which was shaping up beautifully. The church had recently moved into a ginormous new building that had a high tech, burglar alarm system.

When doing production or event work, you have deadlines you must meet. No excuses. To meet those deadlines means sometimes working into or through the night. We requested that the alarm system be changed to go on at a later time so that we could work later. The request was denied, so that meant we had to work faster, and many times without a partner, which was rather dangerous if on high ladders or equipment. Working fervently all day Monday, Tuesday, and Wednesday on the projects was intense and tiring.

On Wednesday, it was time to hang the six enormous 6x10 foot American flags in the church foyer. They were beautiful and proudly displayed American pride. We were working as the mid-week evening service was going on in the sanctuary. There were only two of us hanging the flags, so we were working independently of each other on both sides of the very large foyer. We needed to have all six flags hung by the time service ended, and all ladders were to be removed from the foyer. We were working hard and fast...*too fast.*

I was going up and down a 12-foot ladder, attaching the flags onto the wall at the top, and then running down the ladder to check the straightness of the flags since we were not a two-man team. Working alone, we each had to be up and down the ladder by ourselves. I went up and down the 12-foot ladder maybe four or five times per flag. Time was running out to finish, and I was rushing.

Beauty For Ashes

When I was hanging the last flag, I ran up the ladder the last time and realized my ladder was not at the correct place to tweak the last little detail. I actually walked off the top of the ladder, thinking I was down on the floor. I fell 12 feet down, to a hard marble floor, and in mid-air, I suddenly remembered a tip learned in the Event Safety classes at school: If you find yourself falling off or from something, "Spring, tuck, and roll." Well, while falling 12 feet, I did try to "Spring, tuck, and roll," but I didn't "spring." I simply went *splat* on the marble floor. And since I wasn't able to "spring," I certainly failed to "tuck, and roll!"

I immediately felt a flash of intense heat shoot through my body, from my feet to my neck. Then, just seconds later, went numb from my neck to my feet. I felt nothing, and thought, *Dear Jesus, am I going to be like Joni Eareckson-Tada?*

My friends ran over to me, and I told them that since I didn't have any medical insurance, to just get me some ice, and I would be fine! One friend said, "Uh, I don't think ice is going to fix this Kath; there's a call into 9-1-1 now. Just be still!" Her saying, "Just be still," made me laugh, as I thought: *Gotta stay still; I can't move—even if I wanted to!*

About this time, the evening service was dismissed, and a couple hundred people were surrounding me. Some were crying, some were praying out loud, some were talking with each other sharing sketchy details of the accident, and some were singing in their heavenly language. I don't remember anything else, other than feeling so sad that I had come to bring joy to people I didn't personally know, but sorrow and sadness quickly robbed that joy. Making the matter worse, I hated being a focus of attention.

The call had been made to 9-1-1 and the Nashville Fire Department. The first to arrive was Medical First Alert Responders, with their sirens screaming. The ambulance came soon after, while the first responders did their job and began strapping me onto the spinal board. It appeared that I had possible spinal injuries because I had no feeling in my body—only in my head and face.

I remember that they rolled me out to the ambulance, and there was a lightning storm that night. It was so beautiful. The lightning struck across the sky and lit up the night as though huge, powerful stadium lights were flashing on and off. Enormous, ear-piercing claps of thunder rolled; it was something I had never before experienced in my life. It felt like God was letting me know He was there with me in all His majestic power as rain gently fell on me while I was loaded into the ambulance. It was quite a moment: powerful, huge lightning bolts flashing across the night sky; deafening claps of thunder; and yet, soft, slow motion gentle rain fell on me in the midst of it all.

Arriving at the ER, I felt like I was in a movie—all the rushing about, and immediately sending me for an MRI. After the scan, I was taken back to the ER. A nurse was cutting all my clothes off and I remember feeling embarrassed, asking if she could cover me. Someone else threw a cover of some sort over me.

My pastor friends arrived as I was fighting a bit with the nurse, telling her I didn't want morphine. They explained to me that if the numbness wore off I would be in horrific pain, and they wanted to stay ahead of the pain. I emphatically said, "NO."

In my past, I had had a connective tissue disease, due to a bad TMJ Teflon prosthesis that replaced my TMJ, and it had broken and caused horrible problems that I still suffer from today. On top of all that, I had neuropathy. There was no cure for the connective tissue disease and the only medication that eased all the pain was injectable morphine, which I administered to myself, and to which I eventually became addicted. All that is another story and miracle testimony in itself, however, this was the reason I reacted the way I did at the mention of an injection of Morphine. Eventually, I accepted the injection through the IV, at the prodding of my friends.

The ER doctor came in, and announced that we needed to get a more detailed scan. So, off I went to get a 3-D MRI, still praising God and singing. It was surreal moments of time in which I was experiencing the living God through the Scriptures, like in **John 14:26-27**, where Jesus said: **"But the Counselor, the Holy Spirit, whom the Father will send in my name, will teach you all things and will remind you of everything I have said to you. Peace I leave with you; my peace I give you. I do not give you as the world gives. Do not let your**

hearts be troubled and do not be afraid."

In the wee hours of the morning, after multiple MRIs, I got the prognosis of what had happened to my body after walking off the top of a 12-foot ladder and crashing to the marble floor below.

The doctor said, "Kathlene, we have taken multiple MRIs, and what we see is nothing short of a miracle." He continued, "In falling, your body became a physical human spring through compression! Your calcaneus bones bilaterally have been shattered and pulverized, as though dropping a hard-boiled egg 12 feet onto a cement floor, and your calcaneus bones are the shells on that egg. The miraculous part is not one other bone in your entire body has been broken or fractured. This is not to say the rest of your body did not incur incredible traumatic injuries, which may possibly surface later. For now, we will deal with your heels." As he left, he added, "I will see you some time tomorrow, to discuss options."

My friends and I prayed, praising God, and not understanding any of it. But then again, **Isaiah 55:9** reminded me: **"As the heavens are higher than the earth, so are my ways higher than your ways and my thoughts than your thoughts."** And how can anyone argue with His highest truth? My friends then left the hospital, and I was put into a private room that would become my home for a while.

Later the first day, after the accident, the ankles and calves of my legs began showing perfect zigzag bruises on them. It was the same up the sides of my thighs. I was told that the lumbar section of my back also had zigzag bruising from the compression from when I had hit the floor.

Feeling began coming back into my body, slowly, over the next few weeks. There were only two options for me. One: to have reconstructive surgery on both heels, because they were too shattered to repair. Or, two: to do nothing and let them heal naturally. I decided to go with the "no surgery option" because the reconstructive surgery option had too high of a risk for full recovery. Additionally, multiple surgeries were also part of that prognosis.

I was bedridden, and could put no weight at all on my feet for three months. I was unable to fly home to California because I was a liability to the airlines. Depression began attacking mercilessly, but failed as I claimed victory over it. The airlines told me I could fly home, only if a registered nurse accompanied me, accepting all liability. I could not afford that, but was able to go to my mother's home in North Carolina. She transformed her living room into a hospital room for me, complete with a hospital bed, wheelchair, and lots of windows. North Carolina was beautiful, and my mom was the best caregiver ever!

My days in those four months were filled with much pain, but covered in prayer and time with the Lord in the Word. My friend, Pat Babish, sent me books and CDs, along with weekly Sunday messages that I listened to continually. My son, TJ, sent me comedy movies to keep my spirits up and light-hearted. Friends sent letters, cards, and made weekly phone calls. Exercising in bed was quite the ordeal, and keeping my feet packed in ice was another real hoot, too! Mother and I laughed our way through most of it.

True to the Word in **Proverbs 15:13, "A happy heart makes the face cheerful, but heartache crushes the spirit."** And **Proverbs 17:22, "A cheerful heart is good medicine, but a crushed spirit dries up the bones."**

I was in great physical shape, for which I praised God. My upper body had a lot of hard work to do since I could not move the lower part of my body. Absolutely no weight could be exerted on my feet. My mother, 80 years old, was a little bitty thing and there no was way that she could lift me. It was quite challenging, but I accepted the challenge and won. **Job** encouraged me in **42:2**, when he said to God, **"I know that you can do all things; no purpose of yours can be thwarted."** I was finally able to stand safely four months after the accident.

At that time, Mother flew home to California with me and stayed a week. My daughter, Melody, came to live with me for a few months to help me get acclimated as a disabled person. My recovery consisted of many years. I had to learn to walk again. Doctors continued to tell me that I would probably never be able to walk again, without the assistance of a walker or cane. Extreme caution had to be taken, and I can't tell you how many times I would begin a shopping trip with Melody and get stuck in the back of a store because my feet would just give out on me!

One time, we were in a store and a lady behind me accidentally ran into my heels with her shopping cart. Because the nerves in the back of my heels were exposed, I fell to the floor with horrific pain shooting and ricocheting throughout my body. Even to this day, I have to be extremely careful of getting them hit or bumped. That was certainly a day to remember! Yet, today, I walk perfectly fine, and praise God for it! Now, I must wear heel-less shoes and special orthotics. It is necessary for me to purchase shoes regularly, because any wearing down of the heels will throw my balance off, causing me to fall.

Eighteen months after the accident, our Women's Ministry was having a retreat in Pacific Grove, California. Arrangements were made so that I could attend. One gorgeous day, we were planning a walk on the beach. Walking on sand is actually very difficult for someone physically unstable, but I was determined to go for that walk, and I did. Friends lovingly helped support me on both sides of my body. I spotted five large, smooth stones on the beach and had my friends pick them up for me. Those stones represented to me the same five stones that David picked up, and it only took one of them to slay the giant Goliath. I, too, had a physical giant in my life to slay, and eventually did.

Today, those stones sit in front of a waterfall I have in my home, and they constantly remind me to always remember how fragile life can become in a split second, but with a singular action of God, you can overcome it.

Those were truly the longest, hardest years of my life. The lessons I learned were both physical and spiritual. I have a greater understanding for people who are disabled or physically challenged. When I went places in my wheelchair, many people would speak loudly, as though I was deaf, or they treated me as though I was a helpless child. I learned through that experience that physically challenged people need to be treated with dignity, not pity. They need to be spoken to as though they are whole individuals.

God provided miracle after miracle through that season with finances, medical help, and many other things too numerous to mention. So many times, I almost financially lost my house, yet the favor of God came and saved it many times after my savings had run out.

Six years after the accident, I finally went back to work. I became an art teacher and Elementary Chapel Director at a local Christian school. I loved teaching again, and my spirit soared with passion. I was totally fulfilled as I taught children the love of God, with object lessons that applied to their daily lives—to be overcomers in their world.

If you were to look at me today, you would never guess the story you have just read to be real… but it is. It is my story. Everyone has a story. This is part of my journey, and I am thankful for the power of the Holy Spirit through it all to allow me to uplift and encourage others to live and realize the truth of what **Zechariah** said in **4:6**, to Zerubbabel, about overcoming: **"...'Not by might nor by power, but by my Spirit,' says the LORD Almighty."**

This word is for us today as it was for Zerubbabel back then. It's the only way we will grow into our full potential, purpose, and destiny in God, which is to do it HIS way through the power of the Holy Spirit! Hallelujah!

The accident brought with it many other physical issues that will probably last a lifetime. Fibromyalgia is now ever present in my body. Arthritis has taken up residency, and just last year, I had spine surgery fusing L4 and L5 with two rods inserted—from the wearing of the compression my body experienced during the fall in 2002. Through it all, I have learned to trust in the Lord more. My faith has grown, and my relationship with Jesus would never be what it is now if it had not been for that accident.

God loves us exactly how and where we are, but He doesn't want us to stay that way! The journey is about becoming more like Him: in stature, character, wisdom, and loving people. That takes growth, and it is inevitable that growth never comes without growing pains and truckloads of "fertilizer!"

Currently, there is a song at the top of the charts about being an *overcomer*, and the lyrics speak my experiences clearly; I believe every word of that song. I am an overcomer, and you can be too! Believe and seek the one true and living God with all your heart. He is waiting to talk with you about anything, everything, and wants to spend time with you. He's as close as softly whispering His name: "*Jesus!*"

God Never Ever Gives Up On You

Julie Johnson

"I love the Lord, for he heard my voice; he heard my cry for mercy. Because he turned his ear to me, I will call on him as long as I live."
Psalm 116:1-2

Beauty For Ashes

When I was asked to participate in writing my personal testimony for this book, I did not hesitate to say "Yes!" The Lord has been prompting me for a long time to speak up and write about my relationship with Him. It was not until I began thinking about how I would get this out, that I began to question everything. How will I say it? What will I say? How much do I tell? The following will be only the promptings given to me by God to share with you. I pray that you will find faith if you have none, joy if you have turmoil, peace if you have chaos, or simply that a seed may be planted in you for future cultivation—as it was for me.

I was born in the 1960's in the Bay Area of California. My parents met in college and were married at a young age. They had my brother 19 months before having me. As we were being raised, my parents couldn't decide in which religion to raise us. My father had been raised Catholic in the Philippines, and my mother had been raised Presbyterian in Illinois. Consequently, they decided to bring us up outside of any church. As a matter of fact, we were taught to not talk about politics or religion with anyone.

However, at a very young age, I asked very spiritual questions: "Why is there air?" and, "Who made the stars?" and, "Who's going to die first?" etc. My father would smile and say, "Very good question, Julie," but nothing more than that. So, there were no answers for me, and I was always searching.

My Grandma Carmen (my Father's mother), would

come visit, or we would go visit her, and she always wanted to go to church. I remember, when I was three or four, Grandma took me to her Catholic church in Pasadena, California. It was very hot inside, rather boring, and filled with stand up, sit down, kneel, and sing. People were dressed nicely and smiled at me as I fidgeted and complained to my grandmother. Yet, somehow, I was happy to be there and felt so loved by all the people—especially my Grandma Carmen. My father and mother weren't with us; it was just Grandma, my aunties, and me.

I must have heard a little about God, and heard people say prayers, because, somehow, I knew what to do when my mother had a catastrophic thing happen in her life. She had lost her wallet at the post office. I thought the world was coming to an end. She was so distraught, I was sure it was the end of our lives as we knew it. Therefore, I went to my room, closed the door, climbed up onto my white and purple canopy bed, and began to "pray."

I had no idea what to say, but I got on my knees on the bed, asked God to save my mommy, and find her wallet so that our lives would not be over. I prayed for what seemed like a long time, because I didn't know how to close the prayer. I just remember saying, "Thank you, God, for hearing my prayer. In the name of the Father, Son, and Holy Spirit. Amen."

Suddenly, our doorbell rang, and my mother went to answer it. My room was straight down the hallway from the front door, so I opened my door and peeked out to see who was there. My mother was handed her wallet from a strange man who stated that he had found it at the post office and had come to return it. I saw her look inside, and to her astonishment, all her credit cards, ID, and money were there. She had a huge smile, thanked the man profusely, and then handed him what seemed like every dollar in the wallet as a reward. I don't remember if he kept all the money or even accepted any; I just remember how happy and assured I was that God had answered my prayer.

I didn't think my mother would understand that God was answering my prayer, so I simply skipped back to my room, climbed back up onto my bed and prayed, "Thank You God."

To a Believer, this may not sound so awesome. But for a little girl who didn't know who God was or what prayer could do, it was amazing. I had this feeling that I knew it would be that way from then on, and had such a sense of peace.

Shortly thereafter, I begged my parents to pay for me to take piano lessons. My mother played, my Grandmother Carmen sang, and I loved pretending to play the piano. I began piano lessons when I was in kindergarten, which started a life-long love of music. While at piano lessons, I found out something. There was a song called, "Jesus Loves Me," which, apparently, everyone is supposed to know. I certainly didn't know it. I saw the look of astonishment on the piano teacher's face when I told her I had never heard it. She told me it was a church song that all little children knew, and then listed other Christian children's songs that I should know, but didn't. I decided that this was the right time to state: "We don't talk about politics or religion in our family." She became quiet, and went right back to the piano lesson.

I was glad I didn't have to talk anymore about things that made me feel uncomfortable. It felt good to stand up for my family's beliefs, and quote what I had been quoted. Yet, deep down, I wanted to know the songs because it was so obviously shocking to my teacher that I wasn't a child who went to church and knew the children's Bible songs. I felt left out.

That stopped all future talk of church, the Bible, Christian songs, etc. I noticed that my teacher continued to introduce me to songs that had Christian themes, and I was glad. They were as beautiful as all of the other songs—I believe that all music is inspired by God. One thing I did notice, but did not like after the disclosure of our family's atheism, was the extra love and looks that the teacher would give me. Her daughter, who went to my elementary school, was also extraordinarily nice to me and tried to talk to me. It made me feel weird and different. These memories are what I call "spiritual markers," as they did not mean so much then as they do now, in retrospect to my path in finding Jesus Christ.

The next spiritual marker came when I became very sick in first grade. I came down with some kind of severe eye infection that threatened my eyesight, brain function, and potentially my life. My eye did not respond to the medication that had been given to me. In fact, the infection became worse. My eye would not open and puffed up, causing much pain and a very high fever. My mother took me back to the doctor, and began giving me some medication, which I threw up. Finally, she resorted to administering the medication another way–but not through the mouth! This, too, did not work, and in fact, caused me to be very, very sick.

We eventually found out I was severely allergic to the medication. During that time, I was too weak to stand, eat, go to the bathroom, or even talk. As I lay in my bed, feeling so awful—*heavy* is a better word—I tried to keep my eyes open because I wanted someone to comfort me. Everyone was going on with his or her lives; Dad was at work, Mom was working around the house, and my brother and my friends were at school—where I longed to be. I had been home forever, it seemed.

I continued to lie there, glancing at the kitty cat clock on my wall. The tail was swaying back and forth with every second, and the eyes went back and forth, too. It was hypnotic, and I found myself becoming dizzy with a tremendous headache. I felt sick, alone, and scared. Then, a blinding bright light took over my sight, even as I closed my eyes. I eventually started to feel so light and warm; the headache was gone, and I was floating above my body, looking down at my sick self on my bed. I was only six years old then, and did not understand what was going on. I was scared because I seemed to be traveling so far away from my room—up, up, up into space, and yet I could still see my body lying on the bed.

The next thing I knew, I felt very scared when a winged being came to me and told me it was okay—to relax, let go, and come with it. I think it was a female, but I don't remember. However, I do remember that this winged entity folded its wing around me, and held me as we traveled further away. I was scared, and wanted to go back. But soon, I began to feel more comfortable and without pain.

The winged being started to converse with a greater light entity, which I could not look at; I just knew that I felt very happy, warm, loved, and peaceful. I wanted to stay there. The great light entity was telling my winged escort that it wasn't my time; my work was not yet finished on Earth. At that point, I wanted to stay, but the light entity told me that I needed to go back and finish my work in my family. It was not said in words; all was communicated through thoughts.

Then, the light entity became like a man, and we were looking at each other as he talked with me. He told me that my parents loved me, and that I needed to go back and love them, and let everyone know that God is real. He had me look down at my parents who were sitting at the dining room table. I saw my mother walk into my room, and then she ran out to get my father. They were coming down the hallway and He (God) told me it was now time for me to go back, asking if I was ready.

I felt confused because I loved my parents and wanted to be back to normal with my family, yet I wanted to stay in His presence because it was wonderful, perfect, warm, loving, and right. He must have sensed this and told me He would see me again, along with many others of my loved ones, but that right now, I had to go back and take care of my family business. The next thing I remembered, I was zooming back down, and my spirit felt like it was thrown back into my aching and sick body. I was hot, sweaty, heavy, and weak, yet the headache was going away and my mom and dad were both there, trying to help me wake up.

They looked at me, and I asked if I could get up and go to the bathroom. They were thrilled, because, apparently, I had not been up in a very long time. I thought that I needed to tell them what happened. But instead, I just kept repeating to myself that I would remember what was told to me and that I would love them, be good, serve them, and tell them about God.

It has taken me my whole life to encourage them to accept Jesus and convince them that God is real, and Heaven is real; they are part of my life's mission. I'm not done yet. After all, it took me 20 more years before I made my baptismal commitment to God, and began to follow more closely what He wants of me.

After that remarkable experience, life went back to normal. But, I was given reminders everywhere that God was and is real. When I was in the third grade, I had a friend named Elizabeth. Her family was Catholic, and they lived just down the next street from me. Elizabeth and I played together often. She had a very large family. Her grandmother lived with her, as did her mom, dad, and a multitude of older and younger brothers and sisters.

Another spiritual marker moment was when I was playing with Elizabeth in her home, and stopped in the dining room and stared at the wall. She asked me what was wrong. I asked, "Why do you have a thing hanging on your wall that has a man nailed and bleeding from his hands, feet, and head, on a cross?" Elizabeth said, "I don't know; that's Jesus on the cross. Now, let's go play." But I couldn't leave. I was mortified that this was on their wall, especially in their dining room, where people eat!

Just then, her elderly grandmother noticed me staring, bewildered by this man hanging on a cross on the wall. She told me, "Honey, that's Jesus on the cross. He died for us." I asked her, "If He died for you, why do you want to hang it on your wall to remember this horrible thing?" She kept talking to me calmly, smiling, being peaceful and loving, and said, "Jesus died for all sinners. You're a sinner, and I'm a sinner, and everyone in this family, your family, and all others." By this time, many of Elizabeth's family members were walking up, and it was like a family memorial.

Again, I felt confused, awkward, overwhelmed, and torn. I was in awe and wonder of this Jesus, and the way that Elizabeth's grandmother was talking to me made me feel so comfortable—just like I had felt a couple years back when I was very sick. I simply did not understand the emotions I was feeling. I told them that I had not sinned; I was a good girl. And, I stated once again, "In my family, we don't talk about politics or religion." That was the end of that! I didn't want to go back over there.

However, Elizabeth and I remained good friends, and she would invite me to church. I did not go into the sanctuary, but her family let us play in the park, adjacent to the church. I then felt comfortable enough to talk to Elizabeth about church. I told her that my grandmother had taken me when I was little, but that it had been hot and boring. I thought church was for old people, like our grandmothers.

This started to evoke lots of questions on my part, directed to my parents. Why did we not talk about God, the Bible, Jesus on the cross, and church? It seemed to make my parents very unhappy and uncomfortable, so I didn't ask again. Instead, I was really soaking up the songs that I had learned and continued to learn at piano lessons. I listened to other people talk about God, church, and prayer. One thing I recall about all these Christians I was meeting was that they were calm, loving, concerned, and confident people.

By the time sixth grade rolled around, I had become very involved in musical theater. I began my second musical: *Fiddler on the Roof.* This is a Jewish play, so I was surrounded by Jewish people. The director, many of the actors, and most especially the lady who played my mother in the play, were all Jewish. She invited me to her home for a "potluck" Seder meal. I was allowed to go to the cast party, and my family let me stay alone.

Everyone was talking about the Jews, Jesus,

Christianity, music, church, and many other things that I wanted to know about. They saw how eager I was to learn, and the woman who played my mother in the musical asked me if I wanted to be Jewish. I said, "Oh, yes. I want to go to church with you and be a Jew." All their traditions, family practices, and contemplating of God sounded just perfect for me. She hugged me and said that it was wonderful. I went home after the party and told my parents I had become Jewish. They smiled, laughed, and said, "Wow, that's great."

Of course, that didn't work out, as I had no one to support me in this new spiritual endeavor. At the same time, I had two other friends in school who were Catholic, and I spent lots of time at sleepovers at their houses. Bernadette and her family were so sweet. I practically lived with them. Her father always came into her room and hugged and kissed us both goodnight, and talked about God. There were crosses and spiritual quotes all over the house. I liked it.

My other friend was Karen, and her family had me over multiple times, too. Yet, her family—and Bernadette's as well—never invited me to church. Perhaps I just went home on Sunday mornings to avoid asking my parents about the whole church thing. I did, however, go to a Bible camp with Karen. They sang children's church songs there—some of the same songs my piano teacher had tried to introduce to me. It was lots of fun. But then it was time to take Communion. *I don't belong; I don't know what to do!* was the thought that kept going through my mind.

Karen assured me that it was okay. "They'll never know that you don't know God; just say, 'Amen' after they say, 'The body of Christ.' Then, stick out your tongue, and they will put this thin piece of bread in your mouth." I tried it, and felt official. I was a Bible Camp kid! I wanted to go again, but the opportunity never presented itself.

Many years passed, and I was lost in the business of school, friends, music, and theater. If I wasn't at school playing flute and singing in the choir, I was in the theater learning a new musical. I absorbed myself in all these things as I watched my family slowly fall apart.

My mother and father divorced when I was 13. They told my brother and me on Christmas Eve. I was angry that they had ruined my perfect world, my family, and my Christmas. I kept thinking that now I was going to be the girl who was from a broken family. I blamed my mother, and chose to live with my father.

The day my mother and brother moved out, I had been at school. I came home that day to find half of the furniture and belongings gone, as well as my mom and my brother no longer in our home. It was really happening; my family was no more. My dad had not yet arrived home, so I ran around the house, crying and looking at the half that was missing.

There was a hole in my heart, and I became very upset and depressed. I ran to the kitchen to get a knife to kill myself. I picked up a medium-sized knife from the knife block and held it to my wrist. I was scared. *Would it hurt?* I sank down on the kitchen floor with the knife right on my wrist, trying to think of what was worth living for. Crying…crying.

I don't know why or how I stopped. But, somehow, I just didn't go through with it. Praise God, for He was indeed always there for me, protecting me. The next five years were filled with many things that were not good for a young teenage girl. I was a lost soul. I dabbled in drugs, boys, drinking, stealing, various cults, Ouija boards, and other occult things like astrology, numerology, and tarot cards. I studied Satanism, Buddhism, Mormonism, and tried to understand things that brought purpose, fulfillment, and godliness into my life. I was looking for something to fill the hole that was deeply punctured into my heart.

During my high school years, a group called "Up With People" came to sing and dance for us. This was a group of young people, teens and twenties, who ministered with music and movement, God's positive message of faith, hope, love, and joy. I went to a public school, so I look back in amazement that something like that could have happened. (Must have been my hero and Savior God, again.) I loved them! I loved the music, the wholesome happy costumes, and the people in the group who I talked with before they left our school to move on to their next performance.

Another group came on campus called: *Campus Crusade for Christ*. This was when I received my first mini-Bible. It was pocket-sized with only Psalms and the New

Testament. All my Christian friends recognized how much I liked that, and encouraged me to join the high school Bible study group at lunch. I tried it out a few times. Within a few months, we were told that our Bible group could not meet on school grounds during school hours. I never joined another group. However, I did continue to sing many spiritual songs in my Madrigal singing group, and continued to play and sing those Christian piano pieces I had learned earlier.

As a Madrigal singer, I performed at most of the local churches. It was so fulfilling to me. My Christian friends all thought that I understood everything, but I didn't. I just loved these people who loved Jesus and God. I wanted to know more. I wanted what they had: love, joy, peace, patience, kindness, gentleness, faithfulness, and self-control.

Without God in one's life, and without strong moral values being taught at home, children flounder. I was a good girl, but I didn't always do godly things. When I turned 18, I graduated high school and moved to Los Angeles on my own. Before I left, a couple of my Christian friends asked me to accept Jesus into my heart and make Him my Lord and Savior. I did, but was not sure if I believed it myself, or what I had prayed.

When I reached Los Angeles, I landed two jobs to pay for my apartment, food, car, insurance, and any other expenses. I never went back home because my father had remarried when I was 15, and my mother had remarried when I was 17; both couples had moved away. My brother had also married right out of high school, and started a new life with his young wife. I was so sad and alone. God continued to call me with music on the radio; Amy Grant's "Father's Eyes," and "El Shaddai" were songs I longed to hear daily.

One day, I saw a television evangelist right before Thanksgiving of 1980, and, as I had done just the summer before, asked Jesus into my heart again. Only this time, I did it for me because I meant it—not because of my friends who had wanted me to. However, without a good church to be planted into, I struggled quite a bit. I thank God that He never gave up on me.

I attended several different churches, but they weren't exactly right for me and where I was in my life at that time. God continued to teach me. Ironically, at the same time and unknown to me, my brother was finding God and becoming a strong, born-again Christian. He sent me a birthday card for my 22nd birthday with a beautiful poem: "You Called Me Friend." The poem is about two people at the end of their lives on Judgment Day—one being accepted into a Heavenly reward and the other rejected because she had never accepted Jesus as her Lord and Savior. He told me to read the Bible and become born-again.

I had never owned a Bible other than my pocket Bible from Campus Crusade for Christ. So, since I stayed in hotels while traveling so much of the time for my work, (I was an actress, dancer, make-up artist, model, professional cheerleader, singer, and spokesperson) I took one of the Bibles the Gideons had placed in the drawers. I read it often. It had: Where to look in the Bible when you are: angry, hurt, lonely, sad, scared, etc.

My brother and his wife were then beginning to have children, and I would go visit and see their little girl who sang, "I am the way, the truth and the life, no man shall come to the Father but by me. I'm gonna jump up, touch the ground, turn around, and praise the Lord." *Wow, this little three-year-old child knows more than me*, I thought! My brother asked me if I had been reading my Bible. I said that the Campus Crusade mini Bible had not been complete, so I had taken a Gideon Bible and was reading.

For my next birthday, I received my first Bible ever from my brother and sister-in-law. I started to read it cover to cover.

Then, I started going to a local Catholic church with a few different friends. I loved the Catholic church because I was finally beginning to understand the Cross, Jesus, the Trinity, prayer, and Scripture. I also had a warm feeling that I had felt before, when I had been in God's presence with my grandmother.

I began to contemplate all of the times that God had been there for me. I remembered when He saved me from horrible things—how He had been calling me all my life, and that all I had to do was respond. He was penetrating my heart and soul, and drawing me closer to Himself.

In August of 1981, I saw my future husband for the

first time. We became friends by the end of 1981 and dated on and off, until 1986, when we became seriously involved. My brother told me that I shouldn't consider marrying him unless we were "equally yoked." I asked my brother what that meant, and he told me to find it in the Bible. So, I began reading and looking.

When I finally figured out what it meant, Johnnie and I were about to become engaged. I told him that unless we were equally yoked, our marriage would not work. So, off to church we went. He asked me if I wanted to just run off to Las Vegas and get married. I said, "No, I want to get married in a church, under God's eyes, and with His approval." Johnnie agreed, and we began our Christian pre-marital counseling.

Because we were involved with a Catholic church, we went through the RCIA program to become members of the parish. Then, on April 2, 1988, we were both baptized and confirmed. My Grandma Carmen was our godmother, and we had a seasoned couple as our church sponsors.

One day, while I was at church alone, I asked God if I should marry Johnnie or dedicate my life to serving Him. He answered me clearly that Johnnie and I would do powerful things together. By June of 1988, we were married.

Raised by a mother who believed in and preached the Bible, Johnnie was comfortable and familiar with its teachings. I was a Christian neophyte. I studied, and still do study, the Bible daily to hear from God. I sometimes talk to Him as if He were sitting beside me. I have reached out my hand for Him to hold it. I lift my hands in worship and prayer. I listen to what He has to say to me through Scripture readings, Christian music, and nature; there are so many ways that He communicates through the power of the Holy Spirit. My faith grows more and more each day.

As of today, I have: a husband of 26 years, three teenagers (18, 16, 15), and a church we've attended since moving to our current city in 1999. My children have attended church since they were infants. They have gone to Christian schools most of their lives. They have learned who God is through me and my husband, our church children's ministry, their schools, and the people we surround them with. I've learned so much more about who God is through having my children. I believe that children are blessings from God. As they have learned things in kids' church, so have I. As they have learned at their schools, so have I. And as we go about our family lives, God has taught us all and continues to teach us.

We must simply have a child's attitude to believe and have faith in Him. I have had many rough times in my life since accepting Jesus as my Lord and Savior, and being baptized in the name of the Father, the Son, and the Holy Spirit. Yet, through it all, I have always known that no matter what happens, God will never leave me nor forsake me. He never has and He never will.

"I can do everything through him who gives me strength."
Philippians 4:13

"...as far as the east is from the west, so far has he removed our transgressions from us." Psalm 103:12

"If I speak in the tongues of men and of angels, but have not love, I am only a resounding gong or a clanging cymbal. If I have the gift of prophecy and can fathom all mysteries and all knowledge, and if I have faith that can move mountains, but have not love, I am nothing. If I give all I possess to the poor and surrender my body to the flames, but have not love, I gain nothing.

Love is patient, love is kind. It does not envy, it does not boast, it is not proud. It is not rude, it is not self-seeking, it is not easily angered, it keeps no record of wrongs. Love does not delight in evil but rejoices with the truth. It always protects, always trusts, always hopes, always perseveres.

Love never fails.

But where there are prophecies, they will cease; where there are tongues, they will be stilled; where there is knowledge, it will pass away. For we know in part and we prophesy in part, but when perfection comes, the imperfect disappears.

When I was a child, I talked like a child, I thought like a

child, I reasoned like a child. When I became a man, I put childish ways behind me.

Now we see but a poor reflection as in a mirror; then we shall see face to face. Now I know in part; then I shall know fully, even as I am fully known.

And now these three remain: faith, hope and love. But the greatest of these is love." 1 Corinthians 13: 1-13

I Was NEVER Going To Be "One Of Those Girls..."

Lynda Larsen

" 'For I know the plans I have for you,'
declares the LORD, 'plans to prosper you and
not to harm you, plans to give you hope and a
future.' "
Jeremiah 29:11

Let's start at the very beginning, a very good place to start.

I was born at a very young age. You've probably heard that one before, right? All kidding aside, I'm currently 54 years old. That's hard for me to believe, because I feel like I'm only 32. Isn't that true for MOST people? We feel younger than our age! Well, I'm no exception.

When I entered this crazy world, I was blessed with a mom, a dad, and a sister—who was almost two years old at the time. For the longest time, I was the baby in our family, and I thoroughly enjoyed that status. However, my brother arrived seven years later and took that title from me. What nerve! I became the middle child, but never really felt like a "typical middle child" who's often overlooked. From the time I came out of the womb, I had a BIG personality, which made me difficult to ignore.

I was raised in a pretty traditional family. My mom and dad were married for 45 years before my dad went to meet Jesus. They had what most would consider a happy marriage. Our family did not go to church regularly, and we did not pray together as a family, or speak of heavenly things. I didn't realize that until I was much older.

My aunt and uncle were the regular churchgoers in our extended family. They always offered to pick us up (the kids) and take us to church with them on Sundays, if we wanted to go.

Beauty For Ashes

My older sister *always* wanted to go. She loved church because it fit well with the "rule follower" type of personality she had. I went more frequently when I was old enough to be part of the junior high youth group, because *that* was COOL! My brother liked church too, but not as much as Sissy. My mom and dad went to church on Christmas and Easter, but that was about it. They didn't mind if we went to church, but I don't remember talking to them about what we learned, or our thoughts about Jesus.

When I was 12 years old, I attended a Ken Poure Evangelism event at our church. I can clearly remember feeling the tug on my heart as Ken invited anyone to the front who wanted to live their life for Jesus and accept Him as their Lord and Savior.

I was sitting in my seat, trying to muster up the courage to stand up and walk forward. My legs suddenly felt like they weighed two tons each. All my friends would see me! What would they think? Was I sure? *Jesus, is that really YOU tugging at my heart?* At the end of the song, I went to the front of the room and prayed. I remember that day like it was yesterday, because it was my second birthday! I didn't really understand what it meant to be a Christian, but I knew the decision that I had made that day was very REAL.

I was robustly involved in junior high and high school activities. I was a cheerleader, a teacher's assistant, and an extremely social person. I was an average student academically, and had plenty of friends. My mom and dad were always super supportive parents. They came to school events, watched me cheer, and were my biggest fans. My mom allowed me to have friends over often, and they all loved her. She was the FUN mom.

I am 99% sure I survived my tumultuous first marriage because of the support and self-esteem that was poured into me during my childhood and adolescent years. Without that foundation, I wouldn't be the woman I am today. But I was never gonna be "one of those girls." You know the type I'm talking about? No? Read on.

I was married in 1980, when I was only 20 years old. People married younger in the 70's and 80's, so it seemed. My sister had gotten married, two of my closest cousins had gotten married, and to be completely and brutally honest, I didn't want to be "one of those girls" who ended up being 30 years old and single.

When I think about that now, I laugh. Sure, I thought I loved him, but there were red flags. Big, red flags that I ignored. Red flags that were brought to my attention from my mom and dad, yet I still ignored them. My fiancé had anger management issues, and those issues were evident in his life, on and off the court, field, etc. I noticed those red flags, but I didn't want to be left behind. I wanted to get married like *everyone else*! I was SO young.

We were married for almost 12 years, and were faithful churchgoers. Our son was born in 1982, our first daughter was born in 1983, and our second daughter was born in 1985. I quickly became a mommy to three kids who were five years old and under. *Whaaaaaat?* How did that happen? I'll tell you how it happened!

My husband and I were BOTH horrible at birth control, and I was a "Fertile Myrtle." Boy, did I have my hands FULL. We could not afford to send the kids to Christian school, living on only my husband's income, with lots of mouths to feed. So, we decided that I would homeschool our kids for a few years.

Our marriage was pretty good in the beginning, but started to unravel quickly as the kids got older. I can vividly remember lying in bed one night, thinking about how Angie was only 5 years old, and if I could last 13 more years, I could file for divorce. She would be an adult then, and it wouldn't be as difficult for everyone involved. *Wait.* I wasn't going to be "one of those girls;" what had happened to living happily ever after? The pit that I felt in my stomach that night never left until we were divorced in 1992.

My husband was a control freak, and was verbally abusive. He was physically and verbally abused as a child himself. If he became upset with me, he would take the distributor cap out of our family vehicle when he would leave for work so that I would be forced to stay home. Sometimes, he would decide to bring along our cordless handset so that I could not make any calls, and cell phones were not part of our vocabulary back then.

We separated twice during our twelve years of marriage; I took the kids and moved into my parents' house. We tried Christian counseling both times. We would get back together and things would be good for a few months, but they always returned to the same dysfunctional state shortly after. I was miserable.

I swore I would never be "one of those girls" who got divorced. I believed in the "happily ever after" dream, and I certainly didn't want to disappoint God. About a year before things completely fell apart, my husband told me to get a job. He said that if I wanted my independence, I could have it, but I also had to pay half of the family bills.

Our kids entered public school, and I got a job. I was the office assistant in a construction company, and the only female there. It was there where I met *The Man* who captured my heart, cared about me in ways I had never been cared for, and who was also in a tumultuous marriage that was quickly unraveling. We were two bleeding, broken hearts, looking for love.

At the same time, my younger brother had been diagnosed with a rare disease that affected his immune system. He was in and out of the hospital with different types of pneumonia for five years. When I started working at the construction company, he was IN the hospital more than he was OUT.

The Man asked about my brother frequently. Since I was the only female in the company, I would often meet the crew for lunch at a local eatery. *The Man* and I went to the same church, so we were already friends. He understood me. He complimented me. He was easy to talk to. I needed that—more than I even understood myself. It was easy to justify. I was falling apart, and I needed someone to help me keep the pieces together.

From the deepest part of my heart, I never wanted to be "one of those girls," but that's exactly who I had become. Months later, my husband found out about *The Man* and I, and THAT was the worst day of my life. My husband called *The Man's* wife, my employer, my family, my friends, his family, his friends, our pastor, and anyone else who would listen. He called them to teach me a lesson, and to inform them about my infidelity. My life quickly fell apart.

I moved in with my mom and dad, and the biggest mistake I made that day (in a very unstable, emotional state) was agreeing that the kids could stay there, in our home. *The Man* decided to try and make his marriage work, knowing his wife would forgive him, and he was hopeful that things would change for the better. After all, they had four kids who needed a daddy. But their marriage went from bad to worse, and they eventually divorced, years later.

The next three years were filled with Family Court Services, emergency screenings, meetings with attorneys, child advocates, and endless amounts of paperwork. I remarried almost two years later, bought a house in Tracy, then sold the house in Tracy to pay the attorney fees. We had shared custody, but my youngest daughter was miserable when she was with her dad, and was willing to go through a heart-wrenching custody battle for the chance to come and live with me. The older two kids had always been so compliant—peacemakers—who never wanted to rock the boat. Although I don't think they were happy with the shared custody arrangements, they chose to abide by the rules.

More court, more attorney fees, and more heartache for my youngest child; the judge decided the custody arrangement would stay the way it was. She was devastated, and so was I. When she turned 14 years old though, she decided that, one weekend while she was at my house, she would not be returning to her dad's. Of course, my ex-husband called the police (custody violation), and they took my youngest to a children's shelter because she refused to return to her father's. But God had other plans for her; all the local shelters were full, so they brought her back to my house. I promised I would have her speak with her attorney first thing on Monday morning, and I did.

That was the day my faith in Jesus was restored. After years of feeling like God had abandoned me, I felt like things were looking up. I knew that I had disappointed my heavenly Father when I fell in love with *The Man* and was unfaithful to my husband. The guilt was too much to bear; I was ashamed and had turned away from Him. But He had never left me; I had left Him.

My new husband and I were involved in church, serving, and enjoying a great marriage. I'd love to say we lived happily ever after, but unfortunately, that's not the case. But wait a doggone minute! I was NEVER going to be "one of those girls" who was divorced TWICE! Not me. No. Impossible. Never.

Husband Number Two was almost 18 years older than I. Again, my parents had asked if I was SURE I wanted to marry someone who was that much older. I was in my 30's, and he was in his 50's. At that moment, it didn't seem so bad. However, as the hands of time continued, the difference in age became much more difficult to manage.

We raised five teenage kids together, which is no small feat. But when the kids left, our marriage had become nothing more than "roommate status." We were sleeping in separate beds, due to his snoring, and I was working way too many hours in high tech. Our pastor was preaching a series on marriage, but we had grown so far apart that I didn't even think we could participate in the marriage activities they were asking us to do. We discussed how estranged things had become between us, and agreed it was best for both of us to part ways. We were married for 10 years.

That is NOT where my story ends, though. *Husband Number Two* and I ended our marriage as friends. Our children have remained friends as well. However, the twice-divorced guilt that I carried was unbearable at times. How could God ever forgive me, much less bless me, after being divorced twice? Jesus takes the marriage covenant seriously; how could I ever expect His favor again? Here I was, "one of those girls" I never wanted to be.

Beauty For Ashes

Jesus took me through some difficult times in the years ahead. Dream job. Making $90,000 per year. Laid off. Horrible temporary job. Nervous breakdown. Anxiety attacks. Unemployment. Clarity. New job at a Christian school. Making less than $30,000 per year. How was I going to survive in the Silicon Valley, making that kind of money?

After years of guilt, the veil finally lifted. I realized I was a child of the King who had forgiven me the moment I had asked Him. At the end of my life, will I have to look Jesus in the face and tell Him how sorry I am for being unwilling to make my marriages work? For not taking my marriage vows seriously? I think so, but that's okay! However, I decided NOT to carry that heavy package of guilt around on my shoulders anymore.

I had no idea that God's provision was right around the corner. I prayed specifically that if God wanted me to work at the Christian school (running the before and after school care program), He would need to provide me with a roof over my head that I could afford on the new, much less, salary. I figured out how much that was, and told Jesus.

A few months later, a friend offered to rent me a room in their San Jose home for only $300 per month. That was exactly the dollar amount I had given to Jesus! I lived there for two and a half years. God was not only showing up, but he was showing off!

Then, He provided me a place for me to live, RENT

Beauty For Ashes

FREE! I was able to be the "property manager" of a missionary home in San Jose. The only "catch" was that I had to temporarily "move out" of my place for a week or two at a time when there were "short-term" missionaries who needed a place to stay (two to three times per year).

I was able to help the executor of the home by having garage sales and getting rid of years of accumulated "stuff." I was able to update my place by bartering and trading furniture with friends. And I was able to use some of the garage sale money to buy wall art, outdoor patio furniture, pillows, and furniture covers. I had a friend who was out of work, and needed some money. God provided me with enough to pay her for her time, and to purchase the necessary supplies, so that she could redo the kitchen cabinets.

My heart could not be more grateful or more full of love for my Jesus who never left me or forsook me. He brought me through the hardest of times and rejoiced with me during the happiest moments of my life.

Today? I am living in Hawaii to be closer to my grandkids. My daughter and son-in-law are missionaries there, and recently adopted a sweet, little boy, who is three years old. Their own daughter was born shortly after, who is now three months old.

I left the life that I loved: my job, my family, and my friends, to begin a new journey. I don't know how long I will live there, or what my future holds, but I do know ONE thing: My God will never abandon me or disown me. And even though I am "one of those girls," I am HIS girl, and loved by the King of Kings! Forgiven. Fully restored. God has promised He will take care of my needs, and He has proven that over and over again. I trust Him completely and whole-heartedly as I begin this next chapter of my life. Can I get an Amen?

As I have journeyed through life, there are a few Bible verses that I have held near and dear to my heart. God just might want to use these same verses to speak to your heart as well:

"Finally, brothers, whatever is true, whatever is noble, whatever is right, whatever is pure, whatever is lovely, whatever is admirable—if anything is excellent or praiseworthy—think about such things. Whatever you have learned or received or heard from me, or seen in me—put it into practice. And the God of peace will be with you." Philippians 4:8-9

"A new command I give you: Love one another. As I have loved you, so you must love one another. By this all men will know that you are my disciples, if you love one another." John 13:34-35

So Much Love!

Fernanda Reyes

"Search me, O God, and know my heart:
test me, and know my anxious thoughts. See if
there is any offensive way in me, and lead me in
the way everlasting." Psalm 139:23-24

Beauty For Ashes

This is the real life story of a person who has been constantly transformed from the inside out, by the glory of the One who saves!

First, let me share some memories.

My earliest memory is from when I was five months old. I see my parents smile while I splash in a plastic peach bathtub. The back of my head is warm and secure in my mom's hand, and my dad is all wet. Always smiling directly at me. So much fun and so much love!

Next, I'm five years old.

My dad is back from his three hospital jobs. He hasn't slept, but that doesn't matter to him. We go to the park to ride our little car and play. The rain gets us all wet. It feels wonderful! Still, so much fun and so much love!

I don't know God. Grandma is always talking about how wonderful Jesus is and how much she loves Him, but I only see a God who is unreachable behind a bunch of candles, a mean man behind a dark box, and a book we cannot touch. But the love I receive keeps pouring!

I'm starting to question some things about life and my existence. God, I wonder if You are there.

I'm growing, 11 years old now, and expectations are so high. Love is always present at home. My sister and I are such good friends, and my baby brother is the best. Mom trusts me because I can care for him and watch him anytime I want.

Now, there are three of us on the tickle war against Mom! Dad is amazing; always so composed and gentle, rarely upset, and constantly available for us. He makes the best rice with fried eggs over easy: the only thing he knows how to make. But... Inside, I suffer, and it hurts. What happened to my parents? They haven't spoken to each other in two weeks, except through me.

Mom downloads all her problems on me; somehow I feel important until I am asked to take sides. I don't want to grow up this fast. Can't they see what they are doing to each other...to us? *God, is this how it is supposed to be?* I thought marriage was a magic tale. I thought it would be like Granpa and Grandma, always serving each other and touching and kissing, laughing and joking, and sometimes a five-minute argument that ends on: would you like a cup of coffee with a little cookie? *God, are You there?*

I start to change; my body is different and I feel different. As with every major event, Mom and Dad bring their love and affirmation. This time, Dad and I go on another date. This one is very important: the puberty talk. He tells me what is happening, what to expect, what boys will say, and how and why to stay pure. "Mija, a boy who cares for you will always respect your body and will never ask you for *proof* of your love." I love our talks over shakes and fries. Everything is so open and filled with so much love!

I am not so proud of my next set of memories.

Beauty For Ashes

In my 11th year, my siblings and I have been playing hide and seek for hours with my cousins. We're having so much fun! I go hide in a closet for the 10th time, and my cousin, who is 15, joins me. He tells me he wants to show me something nice and fun, and that I will really like it. I say okay.

A few minutes later, I storm out of the hiding place, unable to talk or cry. I just go home. I am in shock, unable to speak—for a full day, or maybe it was three. When I finally do tell, my cousin can't walk for three days from the punishment he receives, but my nightmares last a whole year. I don't remember asking God why. I think the fear, the shame, and the guilt took over. I see him every day for the next seven years.

I'm 15 and have mastered the technique of manipulation. I no longer have to think or prepare; it's now part of me. Everything I do or say has one purpose: Simply because I want to.

I map the emotions I will make my boyfriend live through today. I take out my paper and draw my plan. First, I'll make him cry, then apologize for crying, and then laugh. Today, I won't fight, but maybe tomorrow. It brings me pleasure. So much control.

At 16, I love school and have made a major achievement. I'm giving a speech to the whole high school on graduation day. I look ridiculous with my face covered to help heal the first and third degree burns I got almost five months ago, but I don't care. Dad and Mom are here!

Beauty For Ashes

I am so loved!

Life is so good, I enjoy everything about it. I'm 19, and my future looks very promising and successful. I keep meeting these nice people who tell me about a cult (in my country, this was considered a cult): Evangelical Christianity. They say it is a religion and is all in the Bible. I refuse to accept it, although I do feel something is missing, and I still wonder about this God and this prophet Jesus. Ah, but I don't need that *now*.

I'm 20.

It is 10:00 p.m., and I cannot sleep. Life is good. I have it under control and the future looks how I want it to, but I still wonder about You, God. *Are You a distant God?* How could that be, with this wonderful world? I can't accept that all of this is just luck. Certainly, some thought must have gone into creating all this beauty and harmony. Am I just a temporary being, a bunch of bones and organs, who will be devoured by worms and mold in my 90's (or 112, if I live as long as my grandparents) with the only goal of procreation? For what purpose?! I hear about this Jesus, but no one can give me facts. "Have faith," they say. "Just believe!" But I don't want to *just believe.*

Are You there?! I thank You for this great life You've given me, but am I supposed to simply exist? There has to be more to life than this. Are You there? I've tried dianetics, spiritism, the pyramids, soul levitation, self-improvement books. Some work, some are very dark, but nothing lasts.

If You are really there, will You reach out and show me that You are real? Can You come down from Your pedestal? Will You transform my life so that I don't have to wear all these masks?

So I can be real, so I can be forgiven, so I can find true happiness, so I can marry someone who can teach me about You if You exist and will accept me for who I am—not what I represent? So I can live a life that is more than just...stuff? So I can be better? So I won't feel empty? *Show me that You really exist!*

Finally, I begin to move along a different path.

I'm 21, now in the USA, and my date is taking me to a Christian church. Imagine how I feel. *I will just listen and be polite so I won't be sucked into this "cult"* is my thought.

I arrive, a little nervous, and hide behind my date. A handsome man comes to welcome me, as do other people. They seem very excited to meet me. I notice they have shining eyes, like with sparkles or the look of water when the sun touches it. I haven't seen this before; mine don't look that way. Alex, my date, has told them about me, I learn later.

The service begins, and guess who is preaching? The handsome man! I thought preachers were supposed to be old, mad, and ugly. I feel something strange and want to cry, but don't know why. They talk about *You*, Jesus. They say that You only actively preached three years to make such an impact! *Hmm... I still need more facts.*

Back in my home country, at 25, I'm reading <u>The Trojan Horse</u>—which my dad recommended. It's not a Christian book, but the story is about a colonel who travels back in time to 12 hours before Jesus died. I read through the night, starting the second book. What is going on? What happened to my capacity to control my emotions? *Don't cry, remember, unless it serves a purpose.*

I need to leave work because I cannot stop crying. This is the third day! What is going on? I'm so overwhelmed with sorrow and regret. How can a man endure so much? I wasn't even born then! I'm sobbing, knowing there is no point in trying to contain it. I attempt to pray, which really is more of a way to demand of You, to fight with You, God. *Why is this happening?!*

My fiancé tells me Pastor Jeff (the same handsome pastor) thinks I have been touched by God's Spirit. It will be great, he says. *Not for me,* I think. I'm the one with no control, unable to stop this massive explosion inside of me. Somehow, I don't want it to stop. I feel for the first time in many years that I can let go and I will be okay. I'm still dealing with all this, but I have a peace and joy I cannot explain. My eyes look different; they look a little cleaner—not like the darkness I saw in them before. I feel lighter and filled with expectation! Somehow, I sense God's presence in a minute way.

I'm 26, and it is my wedding day.

After almost four years, I have come to realize that the guy I'm marrying is the answer to my prayer from when I was 20. We attend church regularly. My husband believes by faith, and as result, all my questions are answered with few facts. I secretly pray that someone in the church will reach out and ask me if I have any questions about the Bible. I read it, and it is truly Aramaic for me.

A few days later, I receive a phone call. "Hi, how are you? I was praying, and you came to my mind. I was wondering if you have any questions about the Bible. I'll be happy to try to answer them." *What?!*

For the next two years, I bombard this wonderful person with questions. She takes all the bullets. Sometimes, there is no answer, but many times there is. I learn that the Bible was written just 35 or so years after Jesus died, so there is only one generation between Him and the Bible. I learn that there are annals from Kings that talk about Him. I learn that Israel and the towns the Bible mentions exist. I learn that there is historical and anthropological evidence of the main scenes from the Bible. I learn that there are some discrepancies in the Bible, but none change the fact that Jesus was here. I learn that Jesus is the only God who gives—no catch, no requirements, no rehearsed performance, no good deeds needed.

I learn to have faith; that I can be forgiven (though the consequences will not disappear), no matter how big my sins. I learn that there is a God and He is not far away, like I thought. I learn that He can be part of every decision I make, that He will direct my path, and when I go astray He will bring me back. I learn to ask for forgiveness for all the cruelty I've inflicted on people, for the manipulations. I learn that there is such a thing as a strong marriage. I learn that I can give grace because I have been given grace.

We continue attending church, now in San Jose. The church also has a handsome pastor with that special light in his eyes, and the church has people wanting to grow in God—just like us.

There is a saying that "time heals everything," but there are situations where that is not true. *Time* doesn't heal, but Jesus does. He heals everything. I had to choose to forgive in order to be free. I healed from the fear, the shame, and certainly the guilt. Now, most of the bad parts of my life are just memories without pain. Only Jesus could give me the power to do this. Through Jesus, I became a new creation; the old is gone and the new has come, just like the Bible says. I'm not defined by what I did or what was done to me. I am a work-in-progress. I want to live by God's Word. It is alive, and I'm proof of its healing power.

I may not have all the facts, but I have the fact that my life was changed, which is a reality no one can argue against. I pray I will always allow Him to keep searching my heart, and to transform me for His Glory, so that I can be a testimony of the greatness of the One and only God who can transform lives and give everlasting peace, forgiveness, and restoration!

About The Authors

Arica Clement

Arica grew up in the Bay Area, and has always had a love of reading and writing. She graduated from San Jose State University. She is happily married to her husband of sixteen years, and they have three beautiful children. Arica loves the Lord, and enjoys going to church and spending time with her family. Reading books and watching movies is what she enjoys doing in her spare time.

Chi Abraham-Igwe

Chi is originally from Nigeria and moved to the United States in 2001. She and her husband have been happily married for sixteen years, and live in San Jose, California with their three children. They worship at Cathedral of Faith. Chi accepted Jesus Christ into her life at 14 years of age.

Kathlene Delgado

Kathlene is a mom to three children and grandma to eight precious grandchildren. She is a retired Children's Pastor; however, she will never retire from the Ministry! Kathlene's desire is to bring hope and encouragement to all, through God's glory, wherever she goes.

Julie Johnson

Julie is married and has three children. She is excited to collaborate with other Christian women on her first, published writing project. She enjoys acting, singing in a Hawaiian worship band, and hiking with her friends and dog.

Lynda Larsen

Lynda spent the majority of her life as a native Californian, until recently, when she moved to the Big Island of Hawaii to be closer to her daughter, son-in-law, and two adorable grandkids. She is an energetic and lively gal who has the best friends and family on the planet! She loves Jesus with all of her heart and prays that God will use this book to bring hope and encouragement to those who read it.

Fernanda Reyes

Maria Fernanda Reyes Cevallos was born in Quito, Ecuador, and moved to the States when she got married eighteen years ago. Currently, she resides in Morgan Hill, California with her sexy, awesome husband and two precious children. She, along with her wonderful parents and siblings, owns a family business. Fernanda loves life!

www.ingramcontent.com/pod-product-compliance
Lightning Source LLC
Chambersburg PA
CBHW071823020426
42331CB00007B/1591